# WINTER, SPRING, SUMMER AND FALL

## A LIFE FROM MOMENT TO MOMENT

A.E. MCINTYRE

# FOREWORD

Transforming experiences strike us with suddenness, but their meanings unfold slowly. Andy's fine book of small poems is faithful to the spirit of this conflict. We have fleeting glimpses of devastating loss, and the persistence of beauty; of fidelity to ancestry amid the constant challenges and redeeming joys of the day. It's a unique, well-wrought window into the workings of a mind.

**ANDREW CALHOUN**
*Warlock Rhymer: An English Translation of Robert Burns' Scots Poems*

# A NOTE FROM THE AUTHOR

The journey of bereavement is long. For me, my own grief journey began just two weeks shy of my fifth birthday, when my father died. All these years later, I have learned that the appreciation of this life, boils down to the grace of each individual moment. In this volume, over a two year period, I tried to capture as many as I could…all with just three lines.

*For me, each poem is sacred. Each poem like a prayer, quietly lifted up to God.*

GIANTS

I remember
When my father died...
And the many giants
Who came to my house,
To hold my mother
When she cried.
And when I asked
The giants about my father,
The giants said
That my father had gone
To a better place,
A place of love
And peace,
Where he would suffer
No more.

The giants called
This place heaven…
And so,
I asked the giants
If I would ever
See my father again.
And the giants answered me
Saying,
That someday, I too
Would go to heaven
To be with God
And my daddy.
And this made me cry
Because I didn't want heaven,
I just wanted my daddy
And I was only
Four years old.

WEST CHESTER, 1995

# PART I
# WINTER

# DECEMBER

1.

A dusting of snow
Just enough —
To cover the fields.

2.

Love visits me,
Each time
I hear my daughter singing.

3.

The fox
Ran the trail.
I stood perfectly still.

4.

We share
These lives together —
Even on the coldest days.

5.

The silent
December moon —
Kept me looking up.

6.

I found
My father's cufflinks.
He is still here.

7.

Such beautiful sadness
So often comes —
In moments of being alone.

8.

Cold at my door,
A fog like a veil.
This absence we know.

9.
We waited
Through the night —
We sat and watched the stars.

10.
If you wait long enough,
The ghosts in the house
Will speak to you.

11.
Ghost of the past
As snow falls down.
We were once so young.

12.
Soon
Sleep will come —
Then so many dreams.

13.
Night comes
With so many thoughts.
Just need to breathe.

14.

The town kept its secrets--
All these quiet lives,
We never even know.


15.

Through snow flurries,
The little sparrow —
Beckoned at my door.


16.

When I felt
His presence —
I knew I wasn't alone.


17.

I woke up
Dreaming of my brother.
Then I remembered, he is gone.


18.

A quick nap
On a cold day.
This quiet life at home.

19.

Overcast skies,

Trees stripped bare.

Red crimson reigned below.


20.

When I saw

The bluebird among the winterberry,

I knew that I was home.


21.

Blaze of sun

Snow all around.

In awe of beautiful things.


22.

A whirling dervish

Spirit or sprite.

I couldn't believe my eyes.


23.

Sledding before Christmas

We took to the hill —

Learned how to fly.

24.

The cardinal
Appeared out of thin air.
I felt so blessed.

25.

On Christmas morning,
Laughter and joy —
Ringing from every room.

26.

Frozen ground
Now we wait.
Another Christmas past.

27.

If I could
Gather together my dead —
What would they think of my life?

28.

Tonight's puppet show
Paper ballerinas,
And a room full of laughter.

29.

I woke up
And cuddled the cat.
This is Sunday morning.

30.

The light within —
Quiet miracles
All around us.

31.

"This wonderful life,"
He thought to himself.
So much possibility.

32.

As darkness fell,
I tried to hurry home —
Shorter days upon us.

33.

Pink winter rose
Defiant blossom —
Hold on against time.

34.

Between Christmas and New Year,
Like getting lost
In familiar woods.

35.

We waited
For New Year,
With homemade noisemakers in hand.

36.

I played with the train set
I spoke to my father —
It is why I believe in God.

JANUARY

37.

At Twelfth Night
We gathered round the fire.
A toast to the coming year.

38.

Autumn kale
Purple and brilliant —
This long after Christmas.

39.

I woke up to snow
And the memory,
Of so many years.

40.

Winter returned,
With all of my
Childhood dreams.

41.

Post-holiday fanfare
Long winter ahead —
We settle in.

42.

A quiet morning
Brought the sun,
And whispers of Persephone.

43.

Frozen world
I held your hand —
Slowly we made our way.

44.

Outside my window
The sheer face of winter —
Was all that I could find.

45.
A lone goose
At evening.
Another sign from the dead.

46.
Christmas past
We feel the absence —
Of old childhood dreams.

47.
Taking down
The Christmas tree.
Peanut butter pinecones for the birds.

48.
A burst of snow
And we remember —
Feelings of pure joy.

49.
My daughter's imagination —
Brought the snowman
To life.

50.

Two hour delay
We went back to sleep.
Turned off the light.

51.

The blue bird
In the branches —
Made my heart leap.

52.

A happy fox
In the snow.
This is living.

53.

In a quiet house
The restlessness comes.
Still so much noise.

54.

Stately old houses,
The passing generations —
All those winter storms.

55.
Heads down
We journeyed on.
One foot after the other.

56.
The fat squirrel eating
We laughed out loud —
This our life together.

57.
Black crow
Cold winter sky.
So many shadows.

58.
Late night sleet,
Morning brought glass —
Watch where you step.

59.
In silence
I closed my eyes —
I could still see his face.

60.

Then winter,
Took its rightful place —
All stood still.


61.

Talk of a big storm
Excitement starts brewing.
We'll see what happens.


62.

Light snow
Gone to ice, then sleet.
Soon comes the rain.


63.

Beauty
Is so often found,
Just by looking up.


64.

Sun emerges
Ice relents.
Winter ebbs and flows.

65.

The tears were real,

Though I hid them from you.

This was love, from one friend to another.

66.

Isolation breeds discontent.

That nagging fear —

That we really are alone.

67.

I wrote down my heart

Beneath the sun and moon.

I loved each and every one of you.

68.

I remembered the snowstorm,

Bright flashes, orange and white —

Home then he was gone.

69.

The winter blues

Stopped by today.

We consoled each other.

70.

Through long silence
Pain comes and goes.
This is the journey.

71.

At the grocery store
People muddled about.
Let's get home fast.

72.

Winter brought
Snow, ice and wind —
A time to hunker down.

73.

Grey sky cover,
We watched the horizon.
Snow may yet come.

74.

Cold, bleak winter
Ground frozen, lifeless —
Window begonias bring hope.

75.

Today I saw a robin
Despite the snow and cold.
Spring will be here soon.

76.

Pennsylvania winter
Will fool you —
When January feels like March.

77.

On warm January days
Get outside,
Put your hands in the mud.

78.

For me,
Each poem was like a prayer —
Quietly lifted up to God.

79.

And temperatures rose —
As winter,
Took a break from itself.


80.

Cold, grey
All stripped bare.
Winter comes for us.


81.

At his deathbed
My father appeared,
Coming through the door.

82.

Cold walk home
But you know these roads,
Memory will follow.

83.

Another storm
Still no snow —
Ground hog saw his shadow.

84.

Little girl laughs
Ballerina dances,
Chasing winter blues away.

85.

Dear brother
I thought I heard you —
Where have you gone?

86.

Soft snow showers
Instant beauty —
So quiet, so still.

87.
The pain is real
Sometimes unceasing —
Now go stand tall.

88.
Skeletal trees
Draw me in.
Beautiful even now.

89.
Lion in winter
Born on this day.
Strength through difficulty.

90.
Life was so beautiful —
But with tears
In my eyes.

91.
February rain
But still winter.
Stuck between worlds.

92.

In the face
Of this unknown,
All I have left are my dreams.

93.

A winter's peace
Our two girls,
Warm, safe and sound.

94.

I prayed so hard,
My heart left broken.
I still don't understand.

95.

Take hold, stand fast
Nightmares happen,
Storms will rise.

96.

You didn't believe me
But I told you —
Monsters are real.

97.
Grief is like a song,
That is always playing
In your head.

98.
Grey doldrums,
Winter drags on —
Hope grows within.

99.
February bewilders
Windy, bone cold —
But still no snow.

100.
Dark cold night
We reached for blankets.
Cuddle up, stay warm.

101.
Winter starlings
A fluttering, black mass.
Here even now.

102.
Such frigid cold
No squirrel today —
Apple slices gone.

103.
Thoughts of a nation,
Historic February cold.
I dream of Kennedy.

104.
It snowed at last
Lent is coming —
Where do I begin?

105.
A sudden white blanket
Rabbit tracks spread out.
So quickly he is gone.

106.
Midwinter bemusement
Cabin fever sets in.
Dirty hands come spring.

107.

Darkness grows
Cold winds howl —
We know the light will come.

108.

Snow covered branches
Height of the storm.
Stay in, stay warm.

109.

The geese
Cleared the house,
Then disappeared before my eyes.

110.

Dogs love us
Even in winter's cold.
Rest well dear friend.

111.

In spite of the cold
I could hear chirping birds —
Spring was on the move.

112.

On colder days,
Shiver then watch the sky.
We will rest come spring.

113.

Eyes open,
Ice fell like rain —
The sound of loneliness followed.

114.

At the train station
It is still snowing —
Weary travelers all around.

115.

In this passing
Dream of sorrows,
I am not alone.

116.

When words fail us,
We had better pay attention...
To all of the reasons why.

117.

In a matter of time
Temperatures will rise —
Trees will be so green.

118.

Like hushed prayers —
The tears
Fell from my eyes.

119.

Quiet house
Storm outside.
You can almost hear the snow.

120.

Deep roots
No less than a miracle,
Who we are within.

121.

The robin returned,
A sign —
Change would come.

122.

Grocery store tulips
Bright, beautiful colors.
Messengers of spring.

123.

Little warrior queen
Loves to challenge her sister.
Born of pith and fire.

# PART II
# SPRING

MARCH

124.

Rain fell heavily,

Through this time of saints.

Soon all will be green.


125.

March arrived

Bringing ice and snow.

Still we wait for spring.


126.

Cold day again

Forecast calls for snow.

Feels like purgatory.

127.

Sidewalk ice skating
Enveloping dense fog —
Late winter dream.

128.

Snow fell,
We put the kettle on.
The garden can wait.

129.

Snowed in again
Maybe for the last time.
Soon daffodils and pansies.

130.

Bright full moon,
Over snow white fields —
Late winter beauty.

131.

March brought
Snow and daffodils.
And a chance to laugh at ourselves.

132.

Brown water and slush
Great thaw upon us.
I knew it wouldn't be pretty.

133.

The rain fell
Blue sky opened —
So much work to be done.

134.

A harsh winter
Yet life does endure.
Green shoots beneath ice.

135.

Heart heavy-laden,
This drab, sepia world.
Hold your head high.

136.

At the wedding
March loomed in the doorway —
Cycles keep repeating.

137.
I found myself thinking of spring,
Trying to chase away
The clouds.

138.
The crows waited
For us to emerge.
They are always watching.

139.
Spring snow arrived
So we stayed indoors.
Rake and spade waiting.

140.
Spring interrupted —
I brought in the potted pansies.
Now we wait for snow.

141.
Some days
The darkness comes.
Winter can feel so long.

142.
Thaw was coming
I could hear running water —
Felt like I could breathe.

143.
Hands in leaves
I stretch downward.
There is the soil again.

144.
Rainy morning
A head full of dreams.
You'll find your way.

145.
Sometimes,
You feel knocked over sideways —
The hurt too much to bear.

146.
Putting things away,
Throwing out old shoes.
Spring cleaning is hard.

147.

When I saw
The snowy egret,
I was happy to be back outside.

148.

A flat of primroses
Late winter snowstorm —
Soon equinox will come.

149.

Beneath brown
Snow laden fields,
Spring was waiting.

150.

The sparrow
Returned once more.
He must know that we are grieving.

151.

I woke up
To the sound of the wind —
A desire to get things done.

152.

Spring showed up,

But not quite as expected.

Time to get to work.


153.

Three days of rain,

Garden went to mud.

Outside looking for crocuses.


154.

On this day,

You were born to us.

I found my father again.


155.

When the rains come

Memory floods in.

Eventually, all is washed away.


156.

Before you leave

You will already be missed.

Safe travels good friend.

157.
Hands in the soil,
Getting the garden ready.
Comfort from routine.

158.
Three flats of pansies
Placed out in the garden.
This is just the beginning.

159.
Living in the moment,
We allow ourselves
To take in miracles.

APRIL

160.
When it rains,
I like to open up the windows—
Then just sit back and listen.

161.
A bright flash of white
Crashing through the thicket.
Bellowing hounds give chase.

162.
Surprised
By passing showers,
The cat went back to sleep.

163.
Clearing the garden
Clearing the mind.
We rise again.

164.
Wanting to help Daddy,
We went out into the garden —
Planted all the flowers.

165.
It is easy to forget
Then I close my eyes —
I remember everything.

166.
In these quiet moments
Stars shine above.
This is why we love.

167.
Two goldfinches
On my way home.
Another sign of hope.

168.

Out in the field
The sky opened up to drizzle.
Everything looked so green.

169.

As my brother
Held my daughter,
Our father's spirit was near.

170.

With all this rain
The flowers we planted —
Will be sure to grow.

171.

Windows open
A soft breeze —
April so beguiles.

172.

Clouds then rain
A little bit warmer.
Still we wait for spring.

173.

Flash of pink buds
Hint of passing blossoms.
Magnolia flowers burst open.

174.

Snapdragons planted
Listening to the rain —
A beautiful day in the garden.

175.

Stand and face the sun
Breathe deeply, in then out —
The spirit calls just listen.

176.

The magnolia blossoms
Ushered in the spring —
Soon they will be gone.

177.

All winter long,
We dreamt of cherry blossoms.
Now they are real.

178.

Gleefully, "Look at that,"
"I see another one over there."
My daughters spotting forsythia.

179.

Great adventures
So often begin--
On pathways lined with flowers.

180.

Out in the garden
Magnolia in bloom.
Promise fulfilled.

181.

Dark clouds gathered,
Spring felt like winter —
Storms happen even now.

182.

Late morning dream,
Dim light, snow on the ground.
The magnolia dropped her blossoms.

183.

The potted begonias
Survived winter indoors.
Finally placed out for spring.

184.

For a brief moment
April masqueraded as March.
The pansies weren't bothered.

185.

Windows open
Damp air cuts to the bone.
The smell of April showers.

186.

Clear night
April so inviting —
Mysterious Venus loves the moon.

187.

Under layers of leaves
Life was still waiting.
Just needed a little sun.

188.

A slight chill in the air,

Flowers stand and bloom.

Green life emerging.

189.

Tending the garden

Beneath an orchestra of birds.

Seek and ye shall find.

190.

Our squirrel returned

Ate the crumbs we left out.

A well-fed acrobat.

191.

White as snow

Gentle little violets —

Mistress of spring.

192.

A simple bouquet,

Pansies in a mason jar.

The beauty of small things.

193.

April brings shadows
Rain and soft flowers.
Springtime is mysterious.

194.

This morning
I spied the robin —
She was enjoying the garden.

195.

Sweet, purple violet
Delicate, little flower.
Warmer days ahead.

196.

Out working in the garden
Crawling around, from bed to bed.
Still so many leaves.

197.

A flash of red
Seen through April showers.
Love on parade.

198.

Sitting by an open window —

Something in the air,

A song came to mind.

199.

Aroma of Mohawk Viburnum

Close my eyes —

I wish it could last forever.

200.

Surrounded by colorful flowers

The little girl laughed —

Magic of spring unfolding.

201.

Life at home

A menagerie of events,

From one day to the next.

MAY

202.
Yellow dogwood
In bloom.
Just as it should be.

203.
At the cemetery
There are daffodils and tulips.
Flowers grow so we remember.

204.
Here but a short time
Then they are gone —
The rhododendron in bloom.

205.
On the playground
My daughters danced in circles.
May had arrived.

206.
Wearing springtime hats,
Our girls waved and smiled.
Holding hands they were off.

207.
Freshly potted petunias
Cheerful in dappled sunshine.
Sweet breeze, dirty hands.

208.
Painting the front porch
Life goes walking by.
Such a pleasant day in May.

209.
Rain fell at last,
The garden could finally breathe.
No need to turn on the hose.

210.

Just like that —
The fragrant viburnum was gone.
All in a flicker of time.

211.

The goldfinch was there
But then, she was gone.
A whirling blur of black and gold.

212.

Dead heading the pansies
I marvel at their tenacity.
All colors fade with time.

213.

A day at the races,
Shoulder to shoulder —
The final push to the line.

214.

Pruning rose bushes
Hoping life will return.
Change brings renewal.

215.
A cat
Making a mess.
This is sometimes what they do.

216.
All the spring flowers
Like so many beautiful words.
They never seem to last.

217.
When she sat alone
Her heart —
Was always singing.

218.
The spiderwort
Appeared in the garden.
Just when I expected it would.

219.
A morning cardinal
High above —
This is why we plant trees.

220.

These secrets
Were all around us.
They were right before our eyes.

221.

The red salvia appeared
Bright red, fearless.
It reminded me of hope.

222.

Rains came —
Our girls sang and danced.
Summer will be here soon.

223.

Watching sailboats,
We dream by the shoreline.
I think all is possible.

224.

I remember
The room in the hospital.
This sadness still comes.

225.

Freshly cut lilac
Placed out in an old vase —
Filled up the entire house.

226.

An unexpected nap,
But a perfect time to rest.
May breezes, warm sun.

227.

Planting peonies
Trying to find a sunny spot.
Now we wait for ants.

228.

When I look into their faces —
I can always find
The past.

229.

God watch over us
Nature our divine goddess,
With summer on the rise.

230.
Walking the dog
My daughters hold the leash.
So many paths to go.

231.
Sitting by the water
Two eagles high above.
You turned and smiled.

232.
When humidity comes
We know that summer is nigh.
Soft rains will follow.

233.
Along the river bank
Train tracks of linear perspective.
Time stands still.

234.
Dividing hostas
A tradition this time of year.
It keeps the garden growing.

235.
Today's call for rain
Heat coming on so fast.
Short spring, long summer.

236.
Sitting beneath the stars
A moment free from chaos.
Our wee girls gone to bed.

237.
When summer comes
Pause to remember…
This weight of memory.

238.
I speak to ghosts
They sat by me all winter.
Hushed whispers, promised hope.

# PART III
# SUMMER

JUNE

239.
Hand in hand
We waded into the water.
A father and his daughters.

240.
This river
If you look closely —
It always appears to be laughing.

241.
After the rain
It felt like we could breathe.
The respite of a new day.

242.

Thunderstorms appeared
Clouds gathered with darkness.
A spectacle to be sure.

243.

The orange wood lily
Elegant in its simplicity.
First sign of summer.

244.

Like it or not
We will grow older.
Bumps and protrusions included.

245.

This early morning
I worked the garden.
My ancestors always with me.

246.

Picking out tomatoes
The girls giggled and smiled.
All the pleasures of summer.

247.
Windows open
Way too early for crickets.
Warm nonetheless.

248.
A cold breeze
At this late hour —
June summer waiting.

249.
The blue jay descended
Grandiose in all his finery.
We stood and watched.

250.
Children rough housing
Getting the housework done.
Normal day in June.

251.
On hot days
The sweat pours down.
Happy to be alive.

252.

Hiking the trail
Dense briars surround us.
Keep pushing through.

253.

In the clearing
We rested awhile.
The hard work had paid off.

254.

The chipmunk appeared
Then disappeared.
I thought I had seen a ghost.

255.

Scarlett red
The cardinal paid us a visit.
Well-fed he flew away.

256.

Cleaning out the cellar
Wreckage of accumulation.
We will feel better later.

257.

Pruning grapevine
A little here, a little there.
Just don't disturb the birds.

258.

Turkey vultures gathered
The deer lay prone —
Brutality in summer.

259.

Out in the heat
We toiled beneath the sun.
Summer had arrived.

260.

Walking the field
The heat bore down.
One step at a time.

261.

The wind kicked up
A tree crashed down.
We huddled close in the dark.

262.
After the storm
We cleared the debris.
Tomorrow comes soon.

263.
Soft rains, then a downpour
A collective sigh of relief —
June washes us clean.

264.
Power, speed, revolutions
We pedal as fast as we can.
Summer waits for no one.

265.
Alone in a quiet house
A bump heard at night.
Shadows haunt me still.

266.
Rainy summer morning
I sat reading to the baby —
We daydream by the window.

267.

The little girl holding flowers,
Just made —
Everything so beautiful.

268.

In fields
Of bright yellow flowers,
All we can do is dream.

269.

A secret garden
Holds —
Such simple pleasures.

270.

The London Plane tree
And the redheaded girl.
Everything grows with time.

271.

Faithful geraniums
On a sunny afternoon —
Quiet days in June.

272.

I hear your voice
It startles me through the day.
I think of you always.

JULY

273.

The squirrel
In the magnolia,
Has everything he needs.

274.

Put anger aside
Pain often comes at night.
New day tomorrow.

275.

Just like that,
June is swiftly behind us.
I can hardly believe it.

276.

In the heat of summer
Men gathered for liberty.
A revolution was afoot.

277.

Looking out the window
Morning glories below —
Bright flowers make you smile.

278.

From high above
Fireworks in every direction.
Rising cheers far below.

279.

One day after fanfare
We return to summer —
With corn growing in the fields.

280.

A menagerie of birds
Descended on the garden.
So many songs.

281.

Out of the thicket
The doe suddenly appeared.
She was like an apparition.

282.

At the butterfly house
The girls danced in wonder.
I thought they would fly.

283.

From where I stood
The cat was on the prowl.
A flutter of wings and paws.

284.

The rabbit leapt out
A frantic scurry ensued.
We were both surprised.

285.

At Sandy Hollow
We sat watching the sun.
Green fields so peaceful.

286.

Hiding out

Beneath the night sky —

Hoping to find shooting stars.

287.

In a quiet house

Thunder shook the sky.

Our girls fast asleep.

288.

The grey catbird

Sat by my window singing.

An unassuming, mocking bird.

289.

We awoke

To the song of cicada.

The return of high summer.

290.

On the beach

The groundhog startled us.

We giggled at our surprise.

291.

We could hear crickets
That sound, so undeniable.
I left the windows open.

292.

Listening to cicada
Again by candlelight —
So much to remember.

293.

Words don't always come
Even late at night.
Try again tomorrow.

294.

Under a moon
Full of laughter,
Summer came to us.

295.

Balancing on a high wire
A mourning dove looks down.
Uncertainty follows.

296.
The cats
In the window.
Such lazy summer days.

297.
A walk in the water,
With mud
Between our toes.

298.
It is beauty
That I will cling to —
Especially on difficult days.

299.
We were once
Someone's dream.
Love brought us here.

300.
Beneath the bridge
A different perspective.
Where water meets land.

301.

Two sisters
An old lineage —
Still so much to learn.

302.

I opened my eyes
To beauty.
She had been there all along.

303.

By the lake shore
Time stood still —
I could have sworn it was a dream.

304.

Me and my shadow
She always keeps pace.
Love of my life.

AUGUST

305.
On this night
A blue moon rises.
Such restlessness.

306.
As summer wanes,
We remember —
How good it is to dream.

307.
Watering the garden
Everything swept clean.
Sun and heat tomorrow.

308.

With everyone asleep
You are left to yourself —
I miss them already.

309.

Bright blooms of summer
Climbing ever skyward.
Trumpeted by the sun.

310.

I saw the black cat
But it lay so still —
I couldn't tell how long.

311.

At the fountain
We threw our pennies.
My wish came true.

312.

Zinnias standing tall
Against a brick red palette.
Ease of summertime.

313.

Drove passed

The river.

Felt your ghost today.


314.

Listening

To cricket and cicada —

I once more remember my place.


315.

With each step

That we take —

There are wonders to be found.


316.

Some days it rains,

Other days, it does not.

Life moves in circles.


317.

In the quiet hours,

I love to watch

My daughters reading.

318.

When tragedy comes
Words lose all meaning.
Seek the center in silence.

319.

Beneath the lily pads,
She thought
She had found her prince.

320.

She stood
Before the gazing pool,
A portal to many worlds.

321.

Washing the dogs
Water everywhere.
Pennsylvania summer.

322.

A cicada nest
Dog days of summer —
Life reemerging.

323.

Together
We watched the clouds.
It felt so good to dream.

324.

Flashlights in hand
We venture into night.
Imagination follows.

325.

Rained again,
A slight chill hit the house.
I held you in my arms.

326.

Tomatoes on the vine
Blue glass shimmering.
Our August summer.

327.

Watching Perseids showers
We cuddled under a blanket.
The sky seemed to fall.

328.

On August nights
September whispers to us.
Even with this warm rain.

329.

Dancing on the porch
She wore butterfly wings.
Then she smiled at me.

330.

Following her sister
They descended into green.
Last days of summer.

331.

Smiling girl
Summer fields.
Maxfield Parrish skies.

332.

Reading the paper
Serenaded by August cicada.
Another quiet Sunday.

333.

Light descended
As we made our way.
Love all around us.

334.

Sun streaming down
Stained glass shimmered.
Prayers given to God.

335.

At the edge
Of the summer field,
A gateway to another world.

336.

Dancing light
Bright sheen of glass.
Late August sun.

337.

Lost
In the dreamscape —
Of a lingering summer sky.

338.

Little blue flower
I see you each summer...
I don't even know your name.


339.

True beauty
Is so often found —
In the miracle of small things.

# PART IV
# FALL

## SEPTEMBER

340.

September fields calling
Light begins to fade.
Everything winds down.

341.

Faith
Is holding onto love,
From one generation to the next.

342.

Chasing the moon
Bright orange symmetry,
Folktales are real.

343.

Gardens of attrition

Plants dying back.

Chrysanthemums will bloom.


344.

First day of school

Nervous smiles abound.

She will be great.


345.

Soaking rains

Arrived at last.

Now go dance in puddles.


346.

In September

We sit in silence.

Let peace be our guide.


347.

At the park

Friends picnicked together.

I thought of Renoir.

348.

Looking for ghosts
We hastily crossed the field.
Autumn had returned.

349.

The crow appeared
Then cawed to us below.
We were not alone.

350.

Along the tree line
A vanishing point.
There mystery begins.

351.

Last night,
The harvest moon--
Come morning, rise again.

352.

Each day
Holiness comes.
Another chance for miracles.

353.

In the passing light,
All things have their place.
September will come again.

354.

It was
A living history.
Love was at the root of it all.

355.

First autumn fire
Lights flickered and danced.
A triumph over shadows.

356.

Quiet and unassuming
September moves along.
Change is all we know.

357.

From the spruce tree
Sounds of unseen rapping.
A ghostly woodpecker.

358.

Waiting for the moon
We sat by the fire —
You laughed perfectly.

359.

So quiet the rain
But ominous the sky.
A new storm on the horizon.

360.

Sunday morning
Laughter from the kitchen.
We rise and smile.

361.

At the bookstore
Hiding out from the rain.
So many possibilities.

362.

Ever so still,
The crumpled deer carcass--
Left at the side of the road.

363.

The squirrel returned
Always up to something.
Laughed when he saw me.

364.

Sometimes
We must try to forget —
Those things we know so well.

365.

After the storm
We went down to the river.
It never looked so high.

366.

Rising from stone
The face of an angel —
My abiding hope.

367.

Sometimes pain returns…
And it's just as extraordinary,
As joy.

368.

Love is all around us
We need only —
Choose to believe.

369.

Two explorers
Discovered a garden.
There was so much to see.

370.

In the blink of an eye
October beckoned.
We cross over together.

# OCTOBER

371.

A slight chill outside
Winds shook the trees.
It must be October.

372.

October brought rain
A sense of eeriness followed.
Imagination begins.

373.

Even in October
We could hear crickets.
Change is inevitable.

374.

In the rush of morning
I held your hand —
We needed no words.

375.

When in doubt
Look to the fields.
The answers will come.

376.

On the swing set
My daughter flew so high.
Growing up too fast.

377.

Sitting in silence
We sought the center.
October waited for us.

378.

At evening time
We cheered the sunset.
Falling light over quiet fields.

379.

As they lay sleeping
We smiled at each other —
This our best creation.

380.

Air grew cold
Out driving old roads.
The specter of shadows.

381.

Despite the cold
We sat beneath the sun.
Warmth of mindfulness.

382.

First frost today
We shivered to the bone.
Time moves us on.

383.

Watching my daughter run,
Such intense joy —
That smile on her face.

384.

Crossing the field
The buck was a phantom.
Then he disappeared.

385.

We saw the fox
Scamper across the road.
The plume of that tail.

386.

Under blue skies
Children ran about.
Such a beautiful Sunday.

387.

With this rain
A sense of restfulness.
Time to go gather dreams.

388.

Autumn hit
The fields,
With folktales and whispers.

389.

Light of autumn
My eyes transfixed.
The silence of leaves.

390.

A scarecrow
In the garden.
A king among the fields.

391.

The black cat
In the window.
Just so much to see.

392.

The specter of ghosts
Until we join them.
Before we forget.

393.

She saw
The field of pumpkins —
Smiled from ear to ear.

394.

An open door

So often leads —

To pathways of imagination.


395.

Darkness comes

The monsters return.

Things do go bump in the night.


396.

Alone in a house

The ghosts

Will always come.


397.

The crow

On the fencepost.

Cast a long shadow.


398.

We relished

These Autumn days,

Full of honey crisp apples.

399.

Chilly October
Pumpkin on the doorstep,
Mischief in the air.

400.

The autumn moon
Cast such an eerie glow —
The cornfields came to life.

401.

In the morning hours
We delight in possibility.
At nighttime, we fear the ghost.

402.

All the brick houses
Pumpkins adorning porches.
October brings us home.

403.

The darkness you feel,
Are the shadows
You know.

404.

A bat

Flying through the house…

Caused everyone to scream.

405.

The dead bat

In the house…

Brought the cat so much joy.

406.

Jumping in leaves

Muse of youthfulness —

Try to remember.

407.

At the Halloween parade

Ghouls and goblins danced.

Now they are fast asleep.

408.

Night of dreams

We must be prepared.

Soon spirits will come.

409.
On Halloween night
Come sit by the fire.
So good to see you again.

410.

New Year upon us
Garden gone to rest.
Only so much time.

411.

A musician
Cast in blue.
Dream melody beneath stars.

412.

Listen to your heart
For each moment is sacred —
Now go follow your dreams.

413.

A father
And his daughters.
This man's life.

414.

This mystery
Dwells at the heart of everything.
It always waits for us.

415.

Sitting with my daughter
Nothing else —
Could make me happier.

416.

When we are willing,
We are capable
Of such beautiful things.

417.

Leaves piled up
The work day done.
Then I heard the wind.

418.

Wind through a window
The mind catches on,
It doesn't let go.

419.

The orange cat
Viewed his world.
It was all a game of chance.

420.

Eyes open,
We take in the world.
Images rise or fall within us.

421.

In the face of doubt
I will choose mystery.
For I believe in miracles.

422.

Waiting for the train
A rising sense of loneliness.
Homecomings are always bittersweet.

423.
Red bittersweet
As the air turned cold.
A sign winter had come.

424.
Extraordinary things
Often happen —
From one moment to the next.

425.
Sitting
In November woods —
Eyes open, watching for ghosts.

426.
A haunted garden
Held the memory,
Of blooming, springtime azalea.

427.
Three
Laughing squirrels,
Make a lot of noise.

428.

Just then,

I heard a crow in the distance.

I knew they would return.

429.

We will join hands

And sing.

Then forget about everything else.

430.

I was the voice

That you would hear —

On quiet, rainy days.

431.

My daughters

Beautiful smile

And I remember happiness.

432.

The blue shadow

Of falling

November skies.

433.

I remembered,
My mother crying alone.
She could speak with the dead.

434.

All these quiet miracles
They are so obvious,
We never see them.

435.

Then late autumn comes
Shadows linger,
And the days slow down.

436.

If we can
Sit through the darkness,
We may just find love.

437.

These dreams
The quiet shelter —
Of fading November light.

438.

Warm November
But nostalgia escapes me —
Time feels so different now.

439.

I sat there writing
With my daughter by my side.
She inspires me always.

440.

The freeze returned
Our gardens died back —
And we were just a little bit older.

441.

My daughters
Are warriors.
Just like their ancestors before them.

442.

On good days
And bad,
I had the woods and the fields.

443.

Holding little hands
A sense of peace,
In a world of chaos.

444.

Standing alone
In the fields--
I could see the face of God.

445.

I closed my eyes
And it felt like summer,
Was just a moment ago.

446.

As dawn breaks,
Nighttime shadows relent.
We begin again.

447.

If nothing else
This peculiar world,
Is always full of possibility.

448.

In beautiful silence,
We reconnect
With ourselves.

449.

If only,
I could quit writing —
But this world is far too beautiful.

450.

From the red wagon
Laughter and singing.
I hoped it would never end.

451.

Restless night
Head full of worry.
Morning comes.

452.

So many
Pathways home —
But this is my favorite by far.

453.

We walk through this life
Constantly tasked,
With connecting, all of the dots.


454.

I often catch myself
Daydreaming.
Some days, it is all that I can do.


455.

In November
We held hands.
Searching for heart-shaped leaves.


456.

Wearing
Blackwatch trews,
And thinking of St. Andrew.


457.

Absence
Made me love,
Even those who didn't care.

458.
Every time
I am finished with writing,
Something new catches my eye.

459.
When all else fails
Keep your feet to the ground.
Follow the calling of your heart.

460.
We move
Across the land.
We feel all that we see.

461.
At the museum
Ideas and impressions.
Philosophy as art.

462.
Three years ago
My wee girls,
Still looked like babies.

463.

In the swirl of chaos
In moments of fear —
Always remember beauty.

464.

Listening intently
To the sound of my daughters laughing.
All my troubles fade away.

465.

Life at home
Is so much
Like joining the circus.

466.

On difficult days
My imagination,
Held the keys to everything else.

467.

These bundles
Of pure joy —
My ever spirited daughters.

468.

I grieve

For people who are gone.

That is why, I love you so much.

469.

Each day

Something new to consider.

Such a great, big world.

470.

When things get hard

I close my eyes,

And I try to think of him.

471.

At the art show

A sea of red, over cerulean blue.

Dreamscape of the mind.

472.

This life

An accumulation,

Of ordinary things.

473.

Change upon us
Winter must come.
Then it will be spring.


474.

Midnight
In a cozy house.
A cat asleep on the bed.


475.

Our little, ginger girls
Giggle, laugh and jump.
They are made of us.


476.

My daughter asked me,
"Where is Papa Bill?"
He is right here, between us.


477.

At eighty-two
My mother is a boxer.
She holds on to every word.

478.

Between you and me,
Angels spoke their names —
Before we ever met.

## ABOUT THE AUTHOR

A poet
Out in the field.
This is what he loves,
This is the world he sees.

A.E. McIntyre lives with his wife Blaire, two daughters, and a bunch of cats and dogs, in Chester County, Pennsylvania. He wrote his first poem, in his seventh grade study hall. He has been living his life without his father, for the last four decades, since January of 1978.